Contents

Chapter 1: The Fading Memories

In the initial part of "The Failed to Remember Prediction," perusers are acquainted with a world near the very edge of progress. The secret world's once-lively recollections of an old prescience are gradually disappearing, leaving its occupants feeling disquiet. Amelia, the hero, winds up tormented by mysterious dreams and sections of failed-to-remember information, drawing her more profoundly into the secret.

As Amelia explores her day-to-day routine, she starts to see exceptional events — a quieted murmur among the seniors, a puzzling image carved onto the sanctuary walls. Startled by the blurring recollections, she looks for comfort in the secret world's tremendous library, expecting to track down replies in the midst of the dusty books and antiquated scrolls.

There, Amelia experiences an old original copy — a vital aspect for opening the prediction's insider facts. As she pores over its pages, she finds parts of a cryptic prediction forecasting a disastrous occasion that compromises the secret world's balance. Understanding the meaning of this disclosure, she sets out on an unsafe mission to comprehend the prediction's actual significance and shield the concealed world from looming destruction.

Joined by steadfast partners, Amelia follows mysterious hints that lead her more profoundly into the secret world's strange regions. En route, they experience difficulties that test their boldness and assurance. In the midst of rich timberlands, deceptive mountains, and supernatural domains, they start to sort out the prescience's divided messages, digging into the secret world's set of experiences to reveal the reality that exists.

As Amelia and her partners face not entirely set in stone to defeat their journey, they understand that the prediction is in excess of an anticipating of destruction — it is a source of inspiration. The destiny of the secret world lies in their grasp, and they should stand up to their feelings of dread, manufacture strong bonds, and embrace the power that lives inside to satisfy the prescience and reestablish harmony in the secret world.

"The Blurring Recollections" makes way for an enthralling excursion loaded up with interest, experience, and self-disclosure. As Amelia and her buddies dive further into the prescience's conundrum, they are pushed forward, their mission turning into a test of skill and endurance to unravel the prediction's importance before the blurring recollections overwhelm the secret world in haziness. The stage is set for an amazing story of fate and assurance as the excursion to reveal "The Failed to Remember Prediction" unfurls.

Chapter 2: An Ancient Scroll

In this part of "The Failed to Remember Prescience," Amelia and her friends set out on a mission to uncover a subtle old lookover that holds the way to translating the prediction's secret insights. Directed by the secretive hints from the original copy found in the secret world's library, they set out on a tricky excursion to an old sanctuary reputed to house the hallowed parchment.

Their way is loaded with deterrents, as they cross through thick backwoods and tough scenes, confronting wild monsters and experiencing confounding watchmen that safeguard the sanctuary's hallowed information. Courageous, Amelia and her colleagues draw upon their aggregate assets and faithful assurance to defeat each challenge that hinders them.

After arriving at the sanctuary's entry, they are met with spectacular engineering and complex images scratched into the stone walls — a demonstration of the sanctuary's significant history and its importance to the secret world. As they adventure further into the sanctuary's internal sanctum, they can feel the heaviness of hundreds of years of insight and secrets encompassing them.

Inside the sanctuary's heart lies the chamber that holds the sought-after old parchment — the way to opening the prescience's maximum capacity. Enthusiastic expectation swirls into the atmosphere as they approach the parchment, aware of its holiness and the significance of their central goal. With fear and stunningness, Amelia tenderly unrolls the parchment, uncovering its antiquated text written in exquisite content.

The language of the parchment ends up being a failed-to-remember vernacular, distant from the secret world's ongoing tongue. As they battle to translate its significance, they draw upon their consolidated information and encounters, sorting out pieces of failed-to-remember legend and old images.

Through vigorous exertion and assurance, Amelia and her mates start to open the parchment's insider facts. It uncovers a progression of enigmas and cryptic sections that give further experiences into the prediction's inclination. Each line focuses on a part of the secret world's set of experiences, winding around an embroidery of prediction and fate that traverses ages.

As the night extends, the gathering submerges themselves in the parchment's significant disclosures, enlightening the secret world's past, present, and the expected future. Each word and image takes on significant importance, interfacing the strings of the prescience's story with the secret world's complex embroidery.

Right now, they comprehend that their journey has just barely started. The old parchment is a passage to additional disclosures, and Amelia and her not entirely settled to proceed with their excursion, regardless of the difficulties that lie ahead. Equipped with recently discovered information and encouraged by the parchment's insight, they get ready to continue onward into the strange domain of "The Failed to Remember Prescience." The old parchment fills in as an encouraging sign, driving them nearer and nearer to the secret world's definitive truth and their fate as gatekeepers of its equilibrium.

Chapter 3: The Prophecy Unearthed

As Amelia and her colleagues proceed with their journey in "The Failed to Remember Prediction," the disclosures from the old parchment move them more profoundly into the core of the secret world's set of experiences. Directed by the enigmatic puzzles and sections, they set off on a mission to uncover the secret world's most consecrated chronicles — the store of failed-to-remember information and old predictions.

Their process takes them to the sacrosanct grounds of the Sanctuary of People of Old, a spot covered in secret and protected by an old request of researchers and soothsayers. Upon their appearance, they are met with both veneration and doubt, for the sanctuary's gatekeepers have long shielded the secret world's most valued privileged insights.

To get close enough to the documents, Amelia and her friends should demonstrate their value, finishing a progression of assessments that challenge their insight, strength, and immaculateness of heart. It is an exhausting trial, yet the gathering's unfaltering assurance and kinship demonstrate their grit, procuring the watchmen's trust.

Inside the consecrated corridors of the files, they are awestruck by the immense assortment of parchments, books, and ancient rarities that annal the secret world's rich history. Each parchment they unwind uncovers parts of predictions, some entwined with their excursion, while others indicate a more extensive embroidery of predetermination yet to unfurl.

As they piece together the dissipated predictions, they find a multifaceted example — a snare of interconnected occasions that rise above time. The predictions anticipate a union of destinies, where Amelia and her buddies are uncovered as critical players in the secret world's destiny.

In a snapshot of disclosure, they run over a prescience that reflects the mysterious dreams tormenting Amelia's fantasies. This prediction discusses a failed-to-remember curio — an old remnant of colossal power — that holds the way to opening the secret world's definitive fate. The gathering understands that this artifact is key to the unfurling prediction and the equilibrium they look to re-establish.

Encouraged by their disclosures, Amelia and her buddies fashion a coalition with the sanctuary's researchers and soothsayers, promising to respect their obligation to the secret world's conservation. Together, they interpret the predictions' implications, winding around a story that enlightens the way ahead.

As they leave the Sanctuary of People of Old, they convey with them the heaviness of freshly discovered information and a feeling of significant obligation. The prediction uncovers privileged insights into the past as well as a dream of the secret world's future — a looming combination of powers that will test their determination and reshape their fates.

Furnished with antiquated insight and limited by their common perspective, Amelia and her mates put forward, realizing that the genuine trial by fire and solidarity lies ahead. The excursion to satisfy "The Failed to Remember Prediction" picks up speed as they set out on a journey to uncover the subtle curio — an artifact that might hold the ability to shape the secret world's destiny until the end of time. The Prescience Uncovered turns into a directing light amidst shadows, pushing them forward into the obscure, where their fates entwine with the actual embodiment of the secret world's presence.

Chapter 4: Guardians of the Past

In this part of "The Failed to Remember Prediction," Amelia and her sidekicks wind up at a junction, confronting a pivotal choice that will decide their jobs as watchmen of the secret world's past and future. As they proceed with their mission to uncover the subtle artifact predicted in the predictions, they experience a hermitic request known as the "Gatekeepers of the Past."

The Watchmen, a gathering of mysterious researchers and history specialists, have committed their lives to save the secret world's old information and curios. Their segregated haven lies profound inside magical backwoods, protected from inquisitive eyes and the desolates of time. Just those considered commendable are conceded admittance, and Amelia's gathering should demonstrate their commitment to the secret world's conservation.

As they approach the Watchmen's space, they are met with a progression of preliminaries intended to test their insight, mental fortitude, and feeling of obligation. Every preliminary draws upon the gathering's one-of-a-kind qualities and difficulties in how they might interpret the secret world's mind-boggling history.

During one preliminary, Amelia and her friends should interpret an old content that uncovers the privileged insights of the secret world's failed to-remember gatekeepers, people who once protected the harmony among light and haziness. The content clues at their ancestors' brave deeds, touching off a feeling of association and mutual perspective inside the gathering.

In another preliminary, they dig into the sacrosanct information on the secret world's natural powers — earth, air, water, and fire. The Gatekeepers survey how they might interpret the basic equilibrium, perceiving that the secret world's harmony depends on the agreeable exchange of these powers.

Amelia and her buddies gain the Watchmen's trust as they progress through the preliminaries and are ultimately allowed admittance to the hallowed documents. Inside the chronicles, they experience old curios and relics, each holding a piece of the secret world's set of experiences.

It is in this blessed spot that they track down the main disclosure — an old guide that focuses on the artifact's area. The guide is loaded up with enigmatic images and questions, and unraveling it will require the aggregate information and experiences of the whole gathering.

Joined by their feeling of obligation as gatekeepers of the secret world's past and future, Amelia and her partners devote themselves to tackling the guide's secrets. They understand that the way forward is difficult, laden with unexpected difficulties, and the weight of liability weighs vigorously upon them.

As they plan to go ahead on the following leg of their excursion, they convey with them the insight and favors of the Gatekeepers of the Past. Their union is presently a demonstration of their obligation to save the secret world's legacy and satisfy the prescience's prediction.

The part finishes with Amelia and her sidekicks remaining at the incline of predetermination, prepared to embrace their jobs as evident watchmen of the secret world's past, present, and future. With freshly discovered assurance and a common feeling of direction, they set off to reveal the slippery artifact that might hold the way to reestablishing harmony and satisfying the secret world's failed-to-remember prescience. "Watchmen of the Past" makes way for an awe-inspiring story of gallantry, penance, and the strength of the human soul as they proceed with their mission to satisfy "The Failed to Remember Prescience."

Chapter 5: The Prophetic Riddles

In this chapter of "The Forgotten Prophecy," Amelia and her companions find themselves entangled in a web of prophetic riddles that lead them on a labyrinthine journey. Armed with the ancient map obtained from the Guardians of the Past, they set forth on their quest to locate the elusive relic that holds the key to the hidden world's fate.

The map's cryptic symbols and riddles prove to be an intricate puzzle, each clue revealing a fragment of the relic's whereabouts. As they traverse diverse landscapes and navigate through hidden passages, they encounter challenges that test their ingenuity and teamwork.

In one instance, they come across an ancient temple shrouded in mist—a place rumored to hold the first clue to the relic's location. The temple's entrance is sealed by an enigmatic door adorned with intricate carvings. It is here that they encounter the first of the prophetic riddles, challenging their ability to interpret ancient symbols and unearth the hidden meanings within.

Drawing upon their collective knowledge and intuition, they decipher the riddle, and the door opens, granting them passage to the temple's inner sanctum. There, they discover an ancient chamber adorned with murals depicting the hidden world's history—a visual testament to the prophetic riddles that await them.

As they proceed deeper into the temple, they encounter more riddles, each linked to the hidden world's elemental forces. The riddles test their understanding of the earth's grounding presence, the air's boundless freedom, the water's ever-changing flow, and the fire's transformative power. Through trial and error, they unravel the prophetic messages hidden within, drawing them closer to the relic's elusive location.

In their pursuit of the relic, they encounter guardians—mythical creatures and ancient spirits tasked with protecting the hidden world's most cherished secrets. Each encounter brings new challenges and insights, as the guardians assess Amelia and her companions' worthiness to proceed on their quest.

With each riddle they solve, they gain a deeper understanding of the hidden world's past, the prophecy's significance, and their intertwined destinies. The journey tests their resolve and strengthens their bonds, forging an unbreakable camaraderie among the group.

As they approach the final leg of their journey, they encounter a formidable guardian—a being of ethereal light and wisdom. The guardian poses a riddle that transcends the boundaries of time and space, requiring them to connect the past, present, and future to unlock the relic's location.

In a moment of revelation, Amelia and her companions decipher the intricate puzzle. The guardian nods in approval, acknowledging their worthiness, and imparts a final piece of advice—a reminder of the hidden world's delicate balance and their pivotal roles in restoring harmony.

Emboldened by their progress and the newfound knowledge, Amelia and her companions set forth, guided by the prophetic riddles, toward the relic's ultimate hiding place. The chapter ends with a sense of anticipation and excitement, as they stand on the cusp of a profound discovery—one that may hold the fate of the hidden world and fulfill "The Forgotten Prophecy." "The Prophetic Riddles" marks a turning point in their journey, as the quest becomes an odyssey of mystery and self-discovery, driving them towards the hidden world's long-lost truths and the relic's elusive embrace.

Chapter 6: Seeking the Seer's Guidance

In this pivotal chapter of "The Forgotten Prophecy," Amelia and her companions embark on a quest to seek the guidance of a legendary seer—the wisest and most enigmatic figure in the hidden world. They have come to understand that the seer holds the key to unlocking deeper insights into the prophecy's cryptic messages and the relic's true significance.

Their journey takes them to the heart of a sacred mountain, where the seer resides in a secluded sanctuary. The path leading to the sanctuary is treacherous, and they encounter mystical creatures and daunting challenges along the way. Each obstacle serves as a test of their determination and commitment to their quest.

Upon reaching the seer's abode, they are met with a sense of awe and reverence. The seer is cloaked in a veil of mystery, his face hidden behind a tangle of long, silver hair. His eyes carry a depth of wisdom that seems to pierce the very souls of those who meet his gaze.

Amelia and her companions present the prophecy's riddles and the ancient map to the seer. With a knowing smile, the seer bids them sit, his voice a soothing melody as he listens to their tale. As he contemplates the riddles and studies the map, he offers cryptic insights into the prophecy's deeper meanings.

The seer explains that the prophecy is not merely a glimpse into the future but a reflection of the past and present—a tapestry woven from the hidden world's collective consciousness. To understand its true implications, they must journey within themselves and embrace the wisdom that lies within their hearts.

Through meditation and introspection, Amelia and her companions delve into their innermost thoughts and emotions. They confront their fears, doubts, and desires, unearthing hidden truths about themselves and their roles in the unfolding prophecy.

The seer reveals that the relic they seek is more than an artifact—it is a symbol of the hidden world's unity, a bridge between the seen and unseen, and a beacon of hope that can restore balance and harmony. Its true power lies not in its physical form but in the collective belief and resolve of those who seek it.

As the seer imparts his wisdom, they realize that the journey to find the relic is not just a quest for a physical object but a spiritual odyssey. They must confront their deepest selves and embrace their interconnectedness with the hidden world, understanding that their destinies are intrinsically linked.

Armed with newfound clarity and inner strength, Amelia and her companions leave the seer's sanctuary with a renewed sense of purpose. The journey ahead is not merely a pursuit of the relic but a quest to restore the hidden world's balance and fulfill the prophecy's deeper meaning.

With the seer's guidance resonating within their hearts, they set forth with unwavering determination. Their bonds are now forged not just by camaraderie but by a shared understanding of the hidden world's interconnectedness and the role each of them plays in its destiny.

As they journey on, they know that the road ahead will be filled with challenges and trials. However, they are prepared to face whatever awaits, knowing that their quest is not just for the hidden world's sake but for their own souls' growth and evolution. "Seeking the Seer's Guidance" becomes a turning point in their journey, shaping their minds and hearts as they embrace their roles as true guardians of "The Forgotten Prophecy."

Chapter 7: Unraveling the Clues

In this chapter of "The Forgotten Prophecy," Amelia and her companions delve deeper into the mystery, piecing together the clues that lead them closer to the elusive relic. Empowered by the seer's guidance and united in their purpose, they embark on a relentless pursuit, determined to fulfill their destiny as guardians of the hidden world.

Following the seer's advice, they journey to a forgotten temple hidden within the depths of an ancient forest—a place rumored to hold the next piece of the puzzle. As they approach the temple's entrance, they are greeted by a magnificent carving that depicts the hidden world's elemental forces in harmonious dance—a reflection of the prophecy's essence.

Inside the temple's dimly lit chamber, they encounter a series of intricate engravings—a visual narrative that unveils forgotten tales of the hidden world's past. Each engraving contains a fragment of the prophecy, weaving a tapestry of interconnected events that span generations.

Amelia and her companions study the engravings, deciphering the symbols and absorbing the wisdom they hold. With each revelation, they gain a deeper appreciation for the hidden world's history and the significance of their quest.

Among the engravings, they discover a series of riddles, each pointing to a specific location within the hidden world. The riddles offer cryptic instructions that challenge their intellect and ingenuity, requiring them to think beyond the obvious and embrace the hidden world's mystical essence.

Undeterred by the complexities of the riddles, the group sets forth to unravel each one. The journey takes them to diverse landscapes—from ancient ruins to crystalline caves and serene waterfalls. Along the way, they encounter the hidden world's diverse inhabitants, each holding a piece of the puzzle.

In their interactions with the hidden world's denizens, they find allies, each sharing tales that add depth to the prophecy's narrative. They learn of forgotten heroes, sacrificial acts, and tales of hope that intertwine with the prophecy's themes.

As they connect the dots, the group begins to see a pattern emerging—one that suggests the relic's location is not a mere physical place but a realm of spiritual significance. They realize that the relic may not be found through conventional means but by tapping into the hidden world's intangible energy and collective consciousness.

With this realization, Amelia and her companions adapt their approach, seeking wisdom not just from the tangible world but from the hearts and minds of the hidden world's inhabitants. Through meditation and introspection, they tap into the hidden world's elemental forces, finding resonance with the prophecy's essence.

As they progress through the unraveling riddles, they grow closer as a group, bonding over shared experiences and revelations. They become attuned to the hidden world's pulse, sensing the relic's presence in the ethereal realms that lie beyond the material plane.

In a moment of enlightenment, they solve the final riddle, culminating in a vision that reveals the relic's true nature. They understand that the relic is not an external object but a source of power that resides within the hidden world and its inhabitants.

Armed with this realization, they emerge from the forgotten temple with renewed purpose and conviction. The journey to fulfill "The Forgotten Prophecy" has taken them on a transformative path, guiding them toward an understanding that the relic they seek is not just an artifact but a reflection of their collective strength and unity.

The chapter ends with the group setting forth on the next leg of their journey, their hearts filled with anticipation and hope. Their quest to restore balance and fulfill "The Forgotten Prophecy" is now fueled not just by a desire for discovery but by a profound sense of connection with the hidden world and its ancient mysteries. "Unraveling the Clues" marks a pivotal moment in their odyssey, one that brings them closer to their destiny as true guardians of the hidden world's past and future.

Chapter 8: The Enchanted Forest's Secrets

In this captivating chapter of "The Forgotten Prophecy," Amelia and her companions venture deep into the heart of the Enchanted Forest—a mystical realm known for its ancient secrets and bewitching allure. Guided by the clues they unraveled in the previous chapter, they believe that the forest holds the next crucial piece of the puzzle—the key to unlocking the relic's true power.

As they step foot into the Enchanted Forest, they are greeted by an otherworldly beauty—a kaleidoscope of colors, enchanted flora, and ethereal creatures. The forest seems to pulse with ancient energy, and an air of anticipation surrounds Amelia and her companions.

They soon discover that the Enchanted Forest is not just a physical place but a realm where the boundary between reality and magic blurs. The forest itself seems alive, its foliage whispering secrets and its glades shimmering with enchantment.

As they delve deeper into the forest's embrace, they encounter mystical guardians—spirits of nature who protect the hidden world's most sacred places. Each guardian tests the group's resolve and understanding of the forest's harmony, ensuring that only those pure of heart may proceed.

Through trials and encounters with the guardians, Amelia, and her companions deepen their bond with the natural world, learning to communicate with the forest's essence. They gain insights into the hidden world's delicate balance, where every action has consequences that ripple through the entire realm.

In the heart of the Enchanted Forest, they find an ancient clearing— a sacred space untouched by time. Within the clearing stands a grand tree—the Tree of Origins—a symbol of the hidden world's ancient roots and its interconnectedness with all living beings.

Amelia and her companions sense that the Tree of Origins holds the final piece of the puzzle. With trepidation and reverence, they approach the tree, their hands gently touching its bark. In a magical surge, they are granted visions—glimpses into the past, present, and future of the hidden world.

Through these visions, they witness the hidden world's creation—a dance of elemental forces and divine magic that birthed the realm and its inhabitants. They also witness the prophecies of the past, glimpses of forgotten heroes who once protected the hidden world from the encroaching darkness.

In the present, they see the consequences of the hidden world's actions—the repercussions of decisions made by generations past. They witness the struggles and triumphs of those who have fought to maintain the realm's equilibrium.

And in the future, they glimpse a vision of hope—a world where the relic they seek has been awakened, restoring balance and bringing forth an era of harmony. They understand that the relic's power lies not in its physical form but in the unity and belief of those who seek it.

The visions granted by the Tree of Origins reaffirm Amelia and her companions' resolve. They know that their quest is more than just a journey for a relic—it is a quest to restore the hidden world's balance and fulfill the prophecy's promise.

With newfound purpose and understanding, they bid farewell to the Enchanted Forest and its mystical inhabitants. They carry the forest's wisdom in their hearts, knowing that the journey ahead will be filled with challenges and trials.

As they venture forth, they are more determined than ever, guided by the Enchanted Forest's secrets and the vision of a united hidden world. They know that the relic they seek is not just a source of power—it is a symbol of hope, the culmination of their shared destiny as true guardians of "The Forgotten Prophecy." "The Enchanted Forest's Secrets" leaves them filled with awe and reverence for the natural world and a profound sense of their place within the hidden world's tapestry of existence.

Chapter 9: A Quest for Truth

In this chapter of "The Forgotten Prophecy," Amelia and her companions embark on a quest for truth—a journey that transcends the physical realm and delves into the hidden world's deepest mysteries. Inspired by the visions granted by the Tree of Origins, they set forth with renewed determination, driven by the belief that the relic they seek holds the key to the hidden world's salvation.

Their quest leads them to a sacred cavern—a place spoken of only in whispers, known as the Oracle's Lair. Within the cavern resides an ancient oracle—an enigmatic figure rumored to possess the wisdom of ages and the ability to peer into the hidden world's cosmic tapestry.

As they approach the Oracle's Lair, an air of anticipation surrounds them. The cavern's entrance is marked by an intricate array of symbols—a testament to the hidden world's intricate interconnectedness. With trepidation and hope, they step into the cavern's depths, their hearts open to the truths that lie ahead.

Upon meeting the oracle, they are met with piercing eyes that seem to see through their very souls. The oracle greets them with a knowing smile, acknowledging their purpose in seeking the relic and fulfilling the prophecy.

The quest for truth begins as the oracle poses questions that dig deep into their hearts and minds. Through introspection and vulnerability, Amelia and her companions lay bare their fears, doubts, and desires. The oracle guides them in understanding the hidden world's cosmic dance—the intricate interplay of light and shadow, creation and destruction, and the ebb and flow of life's cycles.

With each revelation, they find clarity and purpose, their understanding of the prophecy deepening. The oracle reveals that the relic they seek is a manifestation of the hidden world's collective will—a reflection of their unity and resolve to restore balance.

In a moment of profound insight, the oracle imparts the understanding that the relic's power lies not in its physical form but in the intentions and actions of those who seek it. The quest for truth is not about possessing an object of power but embodying the qualities of a true guardian—wisdom, compassion, and the courage to stand against the darkness.

In a series of visions, the oracle shows them glimpses of possible futures—outcomes shaped by their choices and convictions. They see the impact of their actions on the hidden world and its inhabitants, understanding the far-reaching consequences of their quest.

Through the quest for truth, Amelia and her companions gain a deeper appreciation for the interconnectedness of all life and their role as stewards of the hidden world's balance. They realize that their journey is not just about fulfilling a prophecy but about embodying the hidden world's core principles—harmony, coexistence, and respect for all living beings.

With newfound clarity and enlightenment, they bid farewell to the oracle, carrying the truth of their quest within their hearts. As they step back into the world, they know that the journey ahead will be challenging, but they are fortified by the understanding that they are not alone—that the hidden world's ancient wisdom guides them on their path.

The chapter ends with Amelia and her companions embracing their roles as true guardians of truth, united by a shared purpose and determination. They are now prepared to face whatever lies ahead, knowing that the quest for truth is a never-ending journey, one that requires unwavering courage and a commitment to uphold the hidden world's eternal balance. "A Quest for Truth" marks a transformative stage in their odyssey—a stage driven not just by the pursuit of the relic but by the quest to embody the very essence of the hidden world's cosmic tapestry.

Chapter 10: Shadows of Betrayal

In this gripping chapter of "The Forgotten Prophecy," Amelia and her companions find themselves facing a shadowy threat—a betrayal from within their ranks. As they continue their quest to uncover the relic's true power, the hidden world's delicate balance is tested, and the trust among the group is put to the ultimate test.

Amelia and her companions have grown closer throughout their journey, bound by shared experiences and a common purpose. However, as they delve deeper into the hidden world's mysteries, secrets, and personal agendas begin to surface, casting doubt on their unity.

It begins with a series of ominous occurrences—subtle shifts in behavior, cryptic conversations, and the sudden appearance of enigmatic figures who seem to be lurking in the shadows. Amelia's instincts tell her that something is amiss, but she struggles to discern the true nature of the threat.

As the shadows of betrayal deepen, a sense of unease permeates the group. They realize that they cannot let their guard down, for the hidden world's fate hangs in the balance. Trust becomes a precious commodity, and each member of the group must decide whom they can rely on and whom they should be wary of.

Tensions escalate, and emotions run high as suspicions rise. The once-united group now finds itself divided, with each member grappling with their doubts and insecurities. Amelia, as the leader of the quest, bears the weight of responsibility, seeking to maintain unity and harmony among her companions.

Amid the turmoil, they encounter new challenges and adversaries— forces that seem to exploit the group's vulnerabilities and test their resolve. The shadows seem to have a malevolent intelligence of their own as if fueled by the hidden world's darker aspects.

Amelia is confronted with difficult decisions, knowing that the quest's success depends on trust and cooperation. She must navigate through the labyrinth of deception, searching for the truth amidst layers of lies and half-truths.

The chapter unfolds with intense character development, exploring the inner struggles and conflicts each member faces. Friendships are tested, loyalties are questioned, and alliances shift as they grapple with the shadows of betrayal.

Amidst the chaos, Amelia discovers a common thread—an insidious force that seeks to disrupt the quest and claim the relic's power for nefarious purposes. Uniting her companions once more, she urges them to set aside their differences and stand united against the true enemy.

In a climactic confrontation, the group faces the shadows of betrayal head-on, both within themselves and in the form of external threats. Each member must find the strength to confront their doubts and fears, realizing that true unity lies not in the absence of conflict but in their shared determination to protect the hidden world's balance.

As they emerge from the shadows of betrayal, the group undergoes a profound transformation. They understand that their quest is not just about seeking a relic but about overcoming the darkness within themselves and the hidden world.

Reinvigorated by their unity and newfound resolve, they press forward, their trust in one another reaffirmed. The shadows of betrayal may have shaken them, but they have emerged stronger and more committed to fulfilling "The Forgotten Prophecy."

The chapter concludes with a sense of renewal—a turning point in their journey where they have learned that the quest for the relic is not just a physical journey but a test of their character and resilience. The shadows of betrayal have become a catalyst for growth, propelling them closer to their destiny as true guardians of the hidden world's balance.

Chapter 11: Trials of the Forgotten Prophecy

In this pivotal chapter of "The Forgotten Prophecy," Amelia and her companions face a series of trials that test their courage, wisdom, and dedication to fulfilling their destiny as guardians of the hidden world. These trials are not just physical challenges but profound tests of character, pushing them to confront their deepest fears and insecurities.

As they continue their quest for the relic and the fulfillment of the prophecy, they encounter an ancient temple—the Temple of Trials. Legends speak of this temple as a place where true guardians are forged, where the hidden world's champions are chosen to protect its delicate balance.

Entering the temple, they find themselves in a labyrinthine maze— an intricate network of passageways that seem to shift and change. Each member of the group faces a unique set of trials, tailored to their strengths and weaknesses.

For Amelia, the trials force her to confront her leadership and decision-making abilities. She is faced with difficult choices, where the safety of her companions and the hidden world's balance hang in the balance. The weight of responsibility weighs heavily on her, but she finds inner strength in her unwavering commitment to the quest.

For the brooding sorcerer, the trials delve into his past and the darkness that once consumed him. He must face the consequences of his actions and find redemption in the quest's higher purpose. The trials force him to open up, acknowledging that he cannot face the shadows alone.

The wise seer's trials challenge his perception of time and destiny. He must confront his mortality and grapple with the limitations of his powers. Through the trials, he gains a deeper understanding of the hidden world's interconnectedness and the importance of passing on his wisdom to the next generation.

The quirky inventor's trials center around ingenuity and creativity. He is presented with puzzles that test his resourcefulness and ability to think outside the box. Through the trials, he learns that his inventions and ideas can be a source of hope and innovation in the quest to fulfill the prophecy.

As they progress through the trials, they face formidable adversaries and daunting obstacles. Each trial is a reflection of the hidden world's challenges, mirroring the darkness and light that exist within themselves and the realm they seek to protect.

Through perseverance and unity, they overcome the trials one by one. They learn to lean on each other's strengths and support one another in moments of doubt. Their bond as a group deepens, and they come to understand that they are stronger together than they could ever be alone.

At the heart of the temple, they discover the final trial—a test of selflessness and sacrifice. In a climactic moment, they must make a choice that will impact the hidden world's fate forever. It is a moment that tests their understanding of the prophecy's true meaning and the essence of being a guardian.

With courage and conviction, they make the ultimate sacrifice—for the hidden world, for their companions, and for the prophecy's fulfillment. Their actions resonate with the temple's ancient energies, and they emerge from the trials transformed and reborn.

As they leave the Temple of Trials, they know that they have crossed a threshold. The trials have forged them into true guardians, instilling in them a deeper sense of purpose and understanding of the hidden world's cosmic dance.

Filled with newfound wisdom and resilience, they press onward, knowing that their journey is far from over. The trials have shown them that the quest for the relic is not just about obtaining power but about embodying the essence of the hidden world's guardianship.

Chapter 11 marks a turning point in their odyssey, where they have proven themselves worthy of fulfilling "The Forgotten Prophecy." With the trials behind them, they are now prepared to face whatever lies ahead, knowing that their unity and commitment to the hidden world's balance will guide them on the path to their ultimate destiny.

Chapter 12: The Looming Darkness

In this gripping chapter of "The Forgotten Prophecy," a sense of foreboding descends upon Amelia and her companions as they sense the approach of a malevolent force—the looming darkness that threatens to engulf the hidden world. The trials they endured have prepared them for the challenges ahead, but the true test of their strength and unity lies in confronting the shadows that gather on the horizon.

As they continue their journey, they come across ominous signs—a darkening of the skies, unnatural weather disturbances, and a growing sense of unease in the hidden world's inhabitants. It becomes evident that the looming darkness is not a mere metaphor but a tangible force that seeks to consume the realm.

The group senses that the shadows of betrayal they faced earlier were merely a precursor to a greater threat—one that now reveals itself with malevolent intent. They must act swiftly to prevent the darkness from consuming the hidden world and undoing the balance they have fought so hard to protect.

Guided by the seer's wisdom and united in purpose, they follow cryptic clues that lead them to a sacred site—the Nexus of Shadows—a place where the hidden world's delicate equilibrium is at its most vulnerable.

At the Nexus of Shadows, they confront the source of the looming darkness—an ancient malevolent entity that seeks to unmake the hidden world's balance. As they face this formidable adversary, they realize that defeating it requires more than just physical strength— it demands unwavering conviction in the prophecy's fulfillment and the power of unity.

The brooding sorcerer taps into the depths of his powers, finding strength in the belief that he can overcome the shadows of his past. The wise seer draws upon his knowledge of the hidden world's ancient wisdom, understanding that the darkness can only be vanquished through the light of truth. The quirky inventor unleashes his inventive prowess, devising ingenious ways to counter the darkness's malevolence. And Amelia embraces her role as the leader of the group, guiding them with unwavering determination.

In a breathtaking climax, they engage in a fierce battle against the looming darkness—a battle that tests their physical and spiritual fortitude. They draw upon the unity and trust forged through their journey, knowing that the strength of their bond is the key to overcoming the malevolent force.

Through trials and tribulations, they emerge victorious, banishing the darkness back to the depths from whence it came. Their victory is not just a triumph of power but a testament to the hidden world's resilience and the prophecy's enduring truth.

As the skies clear and the hidden world begins to heal from the darkness's grip, the group knows that their quest is not over. The looming darkness was just one manifestation of the hidden world's eternal struggle—the balance between light and shadow, creation and destruction.

Chapter 12 leaves them with a profound sense of purpose and understanding. They now grasp the true nature of their journey—it is not just about seeking a relic or fulfilling a prophecy but about embodying the very essence of the hidden world's guardianship.

As they continue their quest, they carry with them the knowledge that the forces of darkness may rise again. But armed with their unity and the wisdom they have gained, they face the future with courage and hope, knowing that they are the true guardians of "The Forgotten Prophecy." The looming darkness has become a defining moment in their odyssey—a moment that solidifies their commitment to protecting the hidden world's delicate balance, no matter the challenges that lie ahead.

Chapter 13: Whispered Whispers

In this haunting chapter of "The Forgotten Prophecy," Amelia and her companions encounter an enigmatic phenomenon—the Whispered Whispers. These ethereal whispers, rumored to be the voices of ancient spirits, beckon them deeper into the hidden world's secrets and mysteries.

The group stumbles upon an ancient ruin—a forgotten temple veiled in mist and shrouded in secrecy. Within its crumbling walls, they hear faint whispers that seem to call to them, as if urging them to unravel the temple's enigmatic past.

Curiosity and a sense of trepidation lead them further into the temple's heart. With each step, the whispers grow louder, filling the air with an aura of mystique and intrigue.

As they explore the temple's chambers, they discover ancient artifacts and cryptic symbols—an intricate tapestry of the hidden world's history. The whispers seem to resonate from these relics as if the spirits of the past long to be heard and understood.

Amelia, guided by her intuition, senses that the Whispered Whispers hold the key to unlocking a hidden truth—a truth that may alter the course of their quest and the prophecy's fulfillment. Her companions share her conviction, and they delve deeper into the temple's mysteries.

Through the whispers, they gain glimpses of the hidden world's past—forgotten legends, heroic deeds, and tales of valor and sacrifice. The spirits of the past seem to weave a narrative, piecing together the hidden world's ancient legacy.

The Whispered Whispers, however, are not just a font of knowledge but a test of the group's resolve. They must navigate through illusions and illusions of time, as the whispers play with their perceptions and challenge their understanding of reality.

Amelia and her companions must confront their deepest fears and regrets, for the Whispered Whispers have a way of drawing out the hidden world's darkest secrets. In this introspective journey, they gain a deeper understanding of themselves and each other, realizing that their unity is not just based on shared purpose but on compassion and acceptance.

As they reach the heart of the temple, they find an ancient chamber—a portal to the spirits' realm. Here, they encounter the spirits of the past, shimmering apparitions that hold the wisdom of generations. The spirits offer guidance and insights into the hidden world's eternal dance of light and shadow.

Through the Whispered Whispers, they receive revelations about their roles in fulfilling the prophecy. Each member of the group is presented with a choice—a choice that will determine their destiny and the hidden world's fate.

Amelia, empowered by the spirits' guidance, embraces her role as a true guardian, understanding that her leadership goes beyond just guiding the quest—it is about empowering her companions to fulfill their destinies as well.

The brooding sorcerer finds redemption and release from the shadows of his past, embracing the light of hope and a newfound sense of purpose.

The wise seer gains clarity on his role as a keeper of the hidden world's ancient wisdom, realizing that his guidance is essential for the quest's success.

The quirky inventor discovers that his inventive prowess is not just a tool for problem-solving but a means to inspire hope and innovation in the hidden world's darkest moments.

In a powerful culmination, they each make a choice, one that affirms their commitment to the hidden world's balance and the fulfillment of "The Forgotten Prophecy."

As they depart the temple, the Whispered Whispers gradually fade away, leaving them with a profound sense of understanding and unity. They now know that their quest is not just about seeking a relic but about embracing the hidden world's enduring legacy.

Chapter 13 leaves them with a sense of wonder and reverence for the spirits' realm—the realm of the Whispered Whispers—a realm that whispers of timeless wisdom and the eternal dance of light and shadow. As they continue their journey, they carry with them the spirits' guidance, knowing that they are not alone—that the ancient voices of the past walk beside them on the path to fulfilling "The Forgotten Prophecy."

Chapter 14: The Guardians' Test

In this momentous chapter of "The Forgotten Prophecy," Amelia and her companions face the ultimate test of their roles as guardians of the hidden world's balance. Their journey has led them to a sacred sanctuary—the Sanctum of Trials—a place where the true worth of a guardian is measured.

The Sanctum stands tall amidst an otherworldly landscape, surrounded by ethereal mists and a sense of ancient reverence. As they enter the sanctuary, they are greeted by an ancient figure—the Keeper of Trials—a wise and enigmatic being who has overseen the guardians' tests for eons.

The Keeper explains that the Guardians' Test is not just a physical challenge but a profound exploration of their inner selves—their strengths, weaknesses, and convictions. It is a trial of character and resolve, designed to ensure that only those worthy of the hidden world's protection may fulfill "The Forgotten Prophecy."

Each member of the group faces a unique trial, tailored to their individual qualities and virtues. Amelia's trial tests her leadership and the purity of her intentions, for a true guardian, must be driven by selflessness and a deep commitment to the hidden world's harmony.

The brooding sorcerer's trial delves into the shadows of his past, as he must confront the lingering doubts and fears that once consumed him. He must prove that he has overcome his inner darkness and emerged as a true guardian of the hidden world's balance.

The wise seer's trial challenges his wisdom and foresight, testing his ability to decipher the hidden world's intricate tapestry. He must demonstrate that his guidance is grounded in the ancient knowledge and cosmic understanding that the guardians must possess.

The quirky inventor's trial centers around his ingenuity and resourcefulness, as he is faced with inventive challenges that require creative solutions. He must show that his inventions can be a force for good, contributing to the hidden world's prosperity.

As the trials progress, each member of the group undergoes moments of self-doubt and introspection. They are forced to confront their deepest fears and uncertainties, understanding that the path of a guardian is not without its sacrifices and challenges.

Amelia, in particular, is burdened with the weight of responsibility, knowing that the hidden world's fate lies in her hands. Yet, she finds strength in the unity and support of her companions, realizing that the guardians are not just individuals but a collective force of harmony and protection.

Through perseverance and determination, they each overcome their trials, emerging transformed, and validated as true guardians of the hidden world. The Keeper of Trials commends their growth and commitment, acknowledging their worthiness to fulfill "The Forgotten Prophecy."

As they leave the Sanctum of Trials, they do so with a newfound sense of purpose and conviction. They know that the quest to fulfill the prophecy is not just about seeking a relic but about embodying the essence of guardianship—the delicate balance between light and shadow, creation and destruction.

Chapter 14 marks a significant turning point in their journey, solidifying their roles as true guardians. They are now prepared to face the final stages of their quest, knowing that the hidden world's balance and the fulfillment of the prophecy lie within their grasp.

With unity and determination, they press forward, their hearts filled with the wisdom gained from the Guardians' Test. The trials have strengthened their bond and reaffirmed their commitment to protecting the hidden world's delicate dance of existence.

As they continue their odyssey, they carry with them the essence of the Sanctum of Trials—the knowledge that their journey is not just a physical one but a path of self-discovery and spiritual awakening. The Guardians' Test has become a defining moment in their quest, shaping them into the true guardians they were destined to be— guardians of the hidden world's eternal balance and the fulfillment of "The Forgotten Prophecy."

Chapter 15: Echoes of the Past

In this evocative chapter of "The Forgotten Prophecy," Amelia and her companions embark on a journey through time—a mystical encounter with the echoes of the past. Guided by the enigmatic seer and the wisdom of the hidden world, they step into a realm where the barriers of time blur, revealing long-lost secrets and ancient truths.

The journey begins with a series of visions—glimpses of pivotal moments in the hidden world's history. Through the seer's abilities, they witness the rise and fall of civilizations, the birth of prophecies, and the struggles of past guardians who protected the realm's delicate balance.

The echoes of the past lead them to a sacred temple—an ancient repository of knowledge and memories. As they explore its hallowed halls, they are drawn to mystical artifacts and forgotten writings that hold the essence of the hidden world's legacy.

In these echoes, they discover profound insights into their roles as guardians. The past guardians' virtues—courage, compassion, wisdom, and sacrifice—become guiding beacons for the group, inspiring them to embody the same qualities in their quest.

Amelia finds solace and strength in the resilience of the past guardians, knowing that their struggles and triumphs are shared across time. Their dedication to protecting the hidden world's balance reinforces her determination to fulfill the prophecy's promise.

The brooding sorcerer gains a deeper understanding of his journey, realizing that the shadows of his past are not a burden but a testament to his growth as a guardian. The echoes remind him that even in darkness, there is the potential for renewal and redemption.

The quirky inventor's inventive spirit is ignited by the echoes of the past, as he draws inspiration from the hidden world's ancient technologies and innovations. He realizes that his inventions are not just a means to an end but a continuation of a timeless legacy of ingenuity.

The wise seer is profoundly affected by the echoes, for they remind him that his wisdom is not confined to his own time but is connected to the collective wisdom of past and future seers. He discovers that the true power of foresight lies in understanding the hidden world's cyclical nature.

As they delve deeper into the echoes of the past, they also encounter moments of darkness and tragedy. They witness the consequences of imbalance and the price paid when the hidden world's harmony is disrupted.

These echoes serve as cautionary tales, urging them to remain vigilant in their quest. They understand that the hidden world's balance is fragile and that they must not underestimate the malevolent forces that seek to exploit its vulnerabilities.

Through the journey, the group forges a deeper bond with each other and the hidden world's legacy. They realize that they are not just fulfilling a prophecy but continuing a timeless tradition—a tradition of guardians who have protected the realm's delicate dance of existence since time immemorial.

With their hearts and minds enriched by the echoes of the past, they press onward, knowing that the hidden world's fate lies within their grasp. The echoes have become a guiding light in their odyssey, reminding them of the profound responsibility that comes with being true guardians.

Chapter 15 leaves them with a sense of reverence for the hidden world's enduring legacy—a legacy that spans across time and space. As they continue their quest, they carry with them the wisdom of the echoes—the echoes of courage, compassion, wisdom, and sacrifice—that will guide them on the path to fulfilling "The Forgotten Prophecy."

Chapter 16: The Cursed Relic

In this gripping chapter of "The Forgotten Prophecy," Amelia and her companions find themselves face to face with a mysterious and treacherous artifact—the Cursed Relic. Legends speak of its malevolent power and the dire consequences it brings upon those who dare to possess it.

The journey leads them to a hidden chamber deep within an ancient temple—a chamber cloaked in darkness and secrecy. As they approach the relic, a sense of foreboding engulfs them, warning them of the danger that lies ahead.

The Cursed Relic exudes an aura of darkness, emanating energy that taints the very air around it. Its presence is a stark reminder of the delicate balance they seek to protect and the forces that threaten to disrupt it.

Amelia, driven by her unwavering determination, approaches the relic cautiously, guided by the intuition that it holds a vital piece of the prophecy's puzzle. She knows that unlocking its secrets may come at a great cost, but she is prepared to face the consequences.

As she reaches out to touch the relic, a surge of malevolent energy courses through her veins, testing her resolve. The relic's curse attempts to ensnare her mind and corrupt her intentions. But Amelia, fortified by her inner strength and the support of her companions, fights against the darkness, refusing to succumb.

The brooding sorcerer, drawing upon his own experience with the shadows, offers guidance and protection to Amelia. His understanding of the dark forces at play becomes invaluable, as he helps shield her from the relic's malevolence.

The wise seer, with his profound cosmic insight, lends his wisdom to decipher the relic's cryptic symbols and warnings. His guidance is instrumental in unraveling the relic's true nature and the role it plays in the fulfillment of the prophecy.

The quirky inventor, utilizing his inventive prowess, devises protective mechanisms and charms to safeguard the group from the relic's curse. His clever inventions serve as a shield against the relic's corrupting influence.

Together, they navigate through a series of perilous trials and illusions, designed to test their determination and integrity. The relic's curse attempts to exploit their vulnerabilities and sow seeds of doubt, challenging their commitment to the hidden world's balance.

As they unravel the relic's mysteries, they uncover ancient tales of its destructive power—tales of kingdoms torn asunder and lives shattered by its influence. They come to understand that the relic's curse is not just a physical threat but a reflection of the inner turmoil and darkness that resides within those who seek its power.

Through unwavering unity and unwavering conviction, they manage to resist the relic's curse, gradually unlocking its secrets. They discover that the relic is not inherently evil but a manifestation of the hidden world's eternal struggle—a symbol of the balance between light and shadow, creation and destruction.

In a climactic moment, Amelia harnesses the relic's power, not for personal gain but for the fulfillment of the prophecy and the restoration of the hidden world's equilibrium. She embraces her role as a true guardian, understanding that the relic's power must be wielded with utmost caution and responsibility.

With the relic's curse broken, they emerge from the chamber, forever changed by the ordeal. They carry the weight of the relic's dark history and the knowledge that their quest to fulfill "The Forgotten Prophecy" is inexorably intertwined with the hidden world's eternal struggle.

Chapter 16 leaves them with a renewed sense of purpose and a deeper understanding of the hidden world's complexity. They press onward, guided by their unity and fortified by their resilience. The cursed relic becomes a defining moment in their journey—a moment that solidifies their commitment to protect the hidden world's balance and fulfill their destinies as guardians.

Chapter 17: Confronting the Shadow Cult

In this serious part of "The Failed to Remember Prescience," Amelia and her colleagues encounter a vile and imposing enemy — the Shadow Clique. This secret association, covered in dimness and mystery, looks to take advantage of the secret world's fragile equilibrium for its loathsome purposes.

Their process drives them to an old sanctuary concealed profoundly inside the core of a shadowy timberland — the reputed den of the Shadow Religion. As they approach the sanctuary, an emanation of malignance and fear lingers palpably, cautioning them of the peril that lies ahead.

Inside the sanctuary's faintly lit chambers, they experience the Shadow Clique — a gathering of shrouded figures with eyes that appear to pierce through the dimness. The clique's chief, an evil and baffling figure referred to just as the Shadow Expert, uncovers their vile expectations — to tackle the secret politically influential nation for their dim plans.

Amelia, strengthened by her assurance to safeguard the secret world's equilibrium, goes up against the Shadow Expert with resolute determination. She comprehends that this experience isn't simply an actual fight but a conflict of philosophies — a conflict between the longing for power and the obligation to safeguard the domain.

The agonizing magician, drawing upon his encounters with haziness, detects the Shadow Expert's wound thought processes. He realizes that the way of dimness is one of duplicity and misleading commitments, and he cautions his allies to stay cautious against the religion's control.

The astute diviner, with his significant vast understanding, endeavors to dissuade the faction, begging them to embrace the secret world's agreement as opposed to trying to disturb it. His words convey the heaviness of antiquated intelligence, however, he comprehends that the charm of force can daze.

The peculiar innovator, using his creative ability, devises astute techniques and traps to counter the religion's evil plans. His imaginative gadgets become urgent apparatuses in their showdown with the Shadow Clique, assisting with night the chances against their imposing enemy.

In an undeniably exhilarating confrontation, Amelia and her mates take part in a savage fight with the Shadow Clique, a fight that tests their actual ability and their inward strength. They face the faction's dim enchantment, their deceptions, and their constant assurance to hold onto control of the secret politically influential nations.

Amid the bedlam and risk, they stay joined together, every individual from the gathering contributing their special assets to the fight. They comprehend that their solidarity is their most prominent weapon against the Shadow Clique's endeavors to plant dissension and take advantage of their weaknesses.

As the fight arrives at its peak, Amelia defies the Shadow Expert straightforwardly, in a duel of wills and philosophies. Right now, she draws upon the insight acquired from their excursion — the reverberations of the past, the preliminaries of guardianship, and the insider facts of the Reviled Artifact.

With unfaltering conviction, Amelia uncovered the faction's actual aims — to disturb the secret world's equilibrium and dive it into disorder. She reminds the religion that genuine power lies not in mastery but rather in that frame of mind of concordance and the satisfaction of "The Failed to Remember Prescience."

At a strong end, the faction's veneer starts to disintegrate, their dim wizardry debilitating as Amelia's words resound with the insights of the secret world. The Shadow Expert is left shocked and crushed, and the Shadow Clique disintegrates into the shadows from whence they come.

Section 17 leaves them with a feeling of win and help, realizing that they have foiled a huge danger to the secret world's equilibrium. However, they additionally comprehend that the fight isn't finished — that there will constantly be individuals who look to take advantage of the domain's sensitive agreement.

As they leave the sanctuary, they do as such with an increased feeling of cautiousness and assurance. They know that their journey to satisfy "The Failed to Remember Prescience" proceeds, and that facing the Shadow Clique was only one stage in their odyssey.

With their solidarity whole and their motivation built up, they push forward, realizing that the secret world's equilibrium and the satisfaction of the prediction rest upon their shoulders. The showdown with the Shadow Faction turns into a pivotal occasion in their excursion — a second that hardens their obligation to safeguard the concealed world's congruity and safeguard it from the powers of dimness.

Chapter 18: Secrets of the Veiled Path

In this enigmatic chapter of "The Forgotten Prophecy," Amelia and her companions venture deeper into the hidden world, following the trail of an ancient legend—the Veiled Path. This mysterious path is said to hold the key to unlocking the prophecy's final riddles and revealing the ultimate truth that binds the realm's fate.

Guided by cryptic clues from the past, they journey through dense forests, treacherous mountains, and ethereal landscapes—the very heart of the hidden world's secrets. As they traverse the Veiled Path, they encounter enigmatic guardians—spirits of ancient seers who have stood watch over the path for generations.

Each guardian challenges the group to prove their worthiness to tread the Veiled Path—a test of their commitment to the hidden world's balance and their understanding of the prophecy's significance. Amelia and her companions must demonstrate their wisdom, compassion, courage, and unwavering determination, for only those with the purest intentions can navigate the path's mysteries.

The brooding sorcerer finds himself confronting his darkest fears and regrets, as the path delves into the shadows of his past. He must confront the consequences of his choices and find redemption in the face of adversity, proving that his allegiance to the hidden world is steadfast.

The quirky inventor is challenged to rise above his inventive curiosity and desires for recognition, understanding that the Veiled Path demands selflessness and humility. He must show that his inventions are not just tools for personal gain but a means to protect and serve the realm's harmony.

The wise seer faces trials that test his foresight and his ability to unravel the path's intricate symbols and prophecies. He must prove that his cosmic understanding goes beyond mere knowledge and extends to the hidden world's interconnectedness and the grand tapestry of existence.

Amelia, as the leader and guardian of the prophecy, must confront her deepest doubts and insecurities. She faces a series of tests that challenge her leadership, her resolve, and her self-belief. The Veiled Path demands that she not only guides her companions but trusts in their strengths and wisdom as well.

As they progress through the path's trials, they uncover ancient relics and profound secrets, piecing together the hidden world's history and the prophecy's profound significance. Each guardian imparts wisdom and insights that guide them closer to the prophecy's ultimate truth.

Throughout the journey, they also encounter echoes of the past— whispers from the spirits of guardians who have walked the Veiled Path before them. These echoes offer both cautionary tales and encouragement, reminding them of the weight of their quest and the importance of their roles as protectors.

The secrets of the Veiled Path lead them to an ancient chamber—a chamber that holds the final revelation of the prophecy's fulfillment. Here, they are confronted with a moment of truth—a revelation that binds their destinies to the hidden world's eternal dance of light and shadow.

In a moment of profound realization, they understand that the Veiled Path is not just a physical trail but a symbolic journey of self-discovery and enlightenment. The secrets they unveil are not just about the hidden world's past but about the hidden world's future—their future as guardians and protectors.

Chapter 18 leaves them with a sense of awe and reverence, knowing that the path they have trodden is not just a means to an end but a transformative experience. They carry with them the wisdom gained from the Veiled Path—the wisdom that will guide them in the final stages of their quest.

With their spirits strengthened and their bond deepened, they press onward, determined to fulfill "The Forgotten Prophecy" and safeguard the hidden world's delicate balance. The secrets of the Veiled Path become a defining moment in their journey—a moment that cements their commitment to protect the realm and illuminate its path into the future.

Chapter 19: Dance of Shadows

In this mesmerizing chapter of "The Forgotten Prophecy," Amelia and her companions find themselves entangled in a haunting and ethereal realm—the Dance of Shadows. Here, the hidden world's delicate balance is personified in an enchanting dance between light and shadow, creation and oblivion.

Drawn deeper into the realm, they encounter mystical beings known as the Shadow Dancers—ephemeral entities that embody the essence of darkness and light. The dance they perform is not just a spectacle but a reflection of the hidden world's eternal struggle.

Amelia and her companions watch in awe as the Shadow Dancers weave an intricate tapestry of shadows and light, their movements a delicate balance of grace and power. They come to understand that the Dance of Shadows is not just a performance but a profound expression of the hidden world's essence.

As they observe the dance, they are enveloped in a sense of mesmerizing unity, feeling the interconnectedness of all living things within the hidden world. The dance becomes a symphony of emotions and experiences, a testament to the delicate harmony they seek to protect.

The brooding sorcerer, known for his affinity with shadows, feels a profound resonance with the dance. He recognizes that darkness is not inherently malevolent but a necessary counterpart to light—a force that brings balance and contrast to existence.

The quirky inventor, inquisitive as ever, marvels at the dance's intricate patterns and movements. He perceives the dance as a cosmic mechanism—an elegant mechanism that drives the hidden world's cycle of creation and renewal.

The wise seer, with his cosmic insight, perceives the dance's deeper meanings and prophecies woven within the shadows. He discerns echoes of the past and glimpses of the future—a tapestry of destiny that guides the hidden world's course.

Amelia, touched by the dance's ethereal beauty, realizes that the Dance of Shadows is not just a spectacle but a reminder of the hidden world's vulnerability. It shows that the balance they seek is delicate, easily disrupted by malevolent forces and human choices.

In the midst of the dance, they are beckoned to join, becoming part of the symphony of light and shadow. Each companion is paired with a Shadow Dancer, mirroring their movements and emotions, becoming conduits of the hidden world's essence.

Through this dance, they experience profound insights and revelations. They feel the weight of their roles as guardians, knowing that their actions reverberate throughout the hidden world, influencing their destiny.

The Dance of Shadows becomes a transformative experience for Amelia and her companions. They understand that the quest to fulfill "The Forgotten Prophecy" is not just about physical challenges but a spiritual odyssey—a journey of self-discovery and enlightenment.

As the dance draws to a close, they part ways with the Shadow Dancers, carrying with them a deeper connection to the hidden world's essence. The Dance of Shadows becomes a defining moment in their journey—a moment that reaffirms their commitment to protecting the realm's delicate dance of existence.

With renewed resolve and a profound sense of purpose, they press onward, knowing that their quest to fulfill "The Forgotten Prophecy" is imbued with the wisdom of the Dance of Shadows. They carry with them the grace and strength of the dance, guided by the symphony of light and shadow in their pursuit to safeguard the hidden world's eternal balance.

Chapter 20: The Elusive Oracle

In this enigmatic chapter of "The Forgotten Prophecy," Amelia and her companions embark on a quest to seek guidance from the Elusive Oracle—a mysterious and reclusive figure known for possessing profound cosmic insights and foresight.

Their journey takes them to a secluded temple hidden high in the mountains—a place shrouded in mystical veils and guarded by ancient wardens. The temple's isolation and grandeur make it an ideal sanctuary for the Elusive Oracle to commune with the hidden world's secrets.

As they approach the temple, they feel an aura of reverence and trepidation. The temple's ancient walls whisper tales of those who have sought the Oracle's counsel in times of great need, and the profound transformations that have arisen from their encounters.

Inside the temple's hallowed halls, they encounter the Oracle—a figure veiled in shadows and possessing an ethereal aura. The Oracle's eyes, wise and enigmatic, seem to hold the wisdom of countless eons—the knowledge of past, present, and future interwoven.

To gain the Oracle's guidance, they must undergo a series of trials— trials that test not their physical prowess but the purity of their intentions and the depth of their connection to the hidden world.

Amelia faces a trial of self-reflection, where she must confront her inner doubts and fears—acknowledging her vulnerability as a leader and guardian. She understands that her strength lies not just in her determination but in her willingness to acknowledge her vulnerabilities.

The brooding sorcerer is confronted with a trial of empathy, where he must connect with the emotions and experiences of others—something that has always been a challenge for him. Through this trial, he learns the value of empathy and compassion in safeguarding the realm's balance.

The quirky inventor faces a trial of humility, where he must let go of his ego and desire for recognition. He learns that true greatness lies not in seeking praise but in using his inventive prowess to serve the hidden world's harmony.

The wise seer is challenged with a trial of cosmic insight, where he must unravel the hidden world's most cryptic prophecies. He realizes that his abilities are not just a gift but a responsibility—to use his foresight for the greater good and to protect the realm from impending darkness.

Through their trials, they gain a deeper understanding of themselves and their interconnectedness with the hidden world. The trials become a transformative experience, allowing them to shed their old selves and emerge as true guardians—united in purpose and devotion to the prophecy's fulfillment.

Finally, they stand before the Elusive Oracle, seeking answers to the mysteries that have eluded them throughout their journey. The Oracle speaks in riddles and whispers, revealing snippets of prophecy and cosmic truths that guide their path.

The Oracle's guidance is not straightforward, for the hidden world's secrets are woven with intricacies beyond mortal comprehension. Yet, through their trials and their connection to the hidden world's essence, they understand the depth and gravity of the Oracle's words.

As they leave the temple, they carry the Oracle's wisdom with them—a beacon of light in the looming darkness. Their encounter with the Elusive Oracle becomes a defining moment in their journey—a moment that imbues them with the wisdom and foresight needed to confront the prophecy's final challenges.

With their spirits fortified and their bond deepened, they press onward, knowing that the hidden world's destiny rests in their hands. The Oracle's guidance becomes a guiding light, illuminating the path they must tread to fulfill "The Forgotten Prophecy" and protect the realm's delicate dance of existence.

Chapter 21: The Lost City of Mysteries

In this enthralling chapter of "The Forgotten Prophecy," Amelia and her companions set out on an epic expedition to discover the fabled Lost City of Mysteries—a place steeped in legend and rumored to hold the answers to the hidden world's deepest enigmas.

Legends speak of a hidden city, veiled by illusions and guarded by ancient riddles, where ancient knowledge and cosmic truths are said to be preserved. The city is believed to be a repository of the hidden world's accumulated wisdom, waiting for worthy seekers to unlock its secrets.

Guided by the Oracle's cryptic guidance, they journey through treacherous landscapes and ancient ruins, their hearts filled with curiosity and anticipation. Their quest leads them to a dense and uncharted forest—a realm untouched by time, where the boundary between reality and illusion blurs.

As they venture deeper into the forest's heart, they encounter illusions that challenge their perception and understanding of reality. The forest seems to have a life of its own, testing their resolve and unity as they navigate through its mysteries.

Each member of the group faces their illusions, reflecting their innermost desires and fears. The brooding sorcerer must confront shadows from his past, learning to let go of his regrets and embrace the light within. The quirky inventor faces illusions of grandeur and recognition, understanding the importance of humility and selflessness.

The wise seer encounters visions of possible futures, reminding him of the delicate balance of the hidden world and the consequences of their choices. Amelia, too, faces illusions that test her determination and commitment to the prophecy's fulfillment, reminding her of the weight of her responsibilities as a guardian.

As they overcome the forest's illusions, they reach the heart of the Lost City of Mysteries—a grand and ethereal landscape filled with ancient architecture and cosmic symbols. The city seems to emanate an aura of wisdom and enlightenment, resonating with the very essence of the hidden world.

Within the city's labyrinthine streets, they encounter guardians—beings of ancient wisdom and formidable knowledge—who challenge them with riddles and tests of intellect. To gain access to the city's inner sanctum, they must prove their worthiness and the purity of their intentions.

Through trials of wit and wisdom, they earn the guardians' respect, unlocking the city's secrets and delving deeper into its mysteries. The city's knowledge unfolds before them like a cosmic tapestry, revealing hidden truths about the prophecy, the hidden world's origin, and the balance of light and shadow.

They come to understand that the Lost City of Mysteries is not just a physical place but a manifestation of the hidden world's collective wisdom—an embodiment of the struggles and triumphs of those who have sought to protect the realm's harmony.

As they explore the city's sacred halls, they encounter ancient artifacts and cosmic archives—repositories of forgotten histories and prophecies yet to be fulfilled. They realize that their quest to fulfill "The Forgotten Prophecy" is but a part of a grander narrative—a dance of existence that stretches beyond their lifetimes.

In a profound moment of revelation, they grasp the interconnectedness of all living things within the hidden world. The Lost City of Mysteries becomes a beacon of understanding and unity, illuminating the path they must tread to safeguard the realm's delicate balance.

Chapter 21 leaves them with a sense of awe and reverence, knowing that the knowledge they have gained is both a gift and a responsibility. They carry the wisdom of the Lost City of Mysteries with them—a guiding light in the impending darkness.

With their spirits emboldened and their resolve strengthened, they press onward, knowing that the hidden world's fate rests upon their shoulders. The Lost City of Mysteries becomes a defining moment in their journey—a moment that solidifies their commitment to protecting the realm's wisdom and the cosmic truths that bind the hidden world together.

Chapter 22: Into the Heart of Darkness

In this gripping chapter of "The Forgotten Prophecy," Amelia and her companions embark on a perilous journey—venturing deep into the heart of darkness itself. Their quest leads them to confront the malevolent forces that seek to disrupt the hidden world's delicate balance.

Guided by the wisdom of the Lost City of Mysteries, they follow a treacherous path that winds through desolate landscapes and foreboding terrain. The air hangs heavy with an aura of malevolence, and the shadows seem to writhe with malice.

As they press onward, they encounter dark creatures—emanations of malevolence that have been drawn to the shadows' burgeoning power. These creatures are a manifestation of the hidden world's struggles, brought forth by the looming darkness that threatens to engulf everything.

Amelia and her companions must summon all their courage and strength to face these dark adversaries. The brooding sorcerer harnesses the shadows that once haunted him, turning them into a shield against malevolence. He understands that darkness can be a powerful ally when wielded with the intent to protect.

The quirky inventor deploys his inventive creations, using them to counter the creatures' dark magic and illusionary tactics. His resourcefulness and ingenuity become crucial in navigating through the heart of darkness.

The wise seer calls upon cosmic insight to perceive the malevolence's origins and vulnerabilities. He understands that the malevolent forces thrive on fear and uncertainty, and he uses his wisdom to bolster his companions' spirits and resolve.

Amelia, as the prophecy's guardian, bears the heaviest burden. She must confront the darkness within herself, acknowledging her fears and doubts. But she also knows that her commitment to protecting the hidden world is unwavering, and she draws strength from her companions' unwavering support.

As they delve deeper into the heart of darkness, they encounter malevolent illusions and formidable challenges. The malevolence taunts them with their deepest fears and regrets, attempting to sow discord and erode their unity.

Yet, they press onward, refusing to succumb to the malevolence's insidious influence. They understand that their bond is unbreakable, forged through trials and triumphs and that their unity is their greatest weapon against the forces of darkness.

In the heart of darkness, they discover a malevolent nexus—an epicenter from which darkness seeks to spread its influence throughout the hidden world. Here, they must confront the malevolence's embodiment—the Shadow Emissary.

The Shadow Emissary, a fearsome and formidable figure, seeks to exploit the prophecy's fulfillment for its malevolent designs. It embodies the very essence of darkness, seeking to plunge the hidden world into eternal shadow.

In a climactic battle, Amelia and her companions engage in a fierce confrontation with the Shadow Emissary, a battle that tests their physical prowess and their inner strength. They draw upon the wisdom gained from their journey—the echoes of the past, the guidance of the Oracle, and the secrets of the Lost City of Mysteries.

Amidst the chaos and danger, they remain united, each member of the group contributing their unique strengths to the battle. They understand that their unity is their greatest weapon against the Shadow Emissary's attempts to divide and conquer.

As the battle reaches its zenith, they draw upon the hidden world's essence—the dance of light and shadow within themselves. They remember the Dance of Shadows and its profound message—the delicate balance of existence that they must protect.

In a moment of breathtaking valor, Amelia faces the Shadow Emissary head-on, her unwavering commitment to the prophecy's fulfillment and the realm's balance propelling her forward. The battle becomes a dance of light and shadow—a dance that will determine the hidden world's destiny.

Chapter 22 leaves them on the precipice of an epic showdown—the culmination of their journey. They know that they stand at the threshold of the prophecy's fulfillment and that the heart of darkness holds both the greatest dangers and the most profound revelations.

With their spirits steeled and their bond fortified, they press forward, knowing that the heart of darkness is the final crucible in their quest to safeguard the realm's delicate dance of existence. The battle with the Shadow Emissary becomes a defining moment in their journey—a moment that will determine the fate of the hidden world and its eternal dance of light and shadow.

Chapter 23: Breaking the Veil

In this climactic section of "The Failed to Remember Prediction," Amelia and her friends stand near the precarious edge of breaking the cover that covers the secret world in murkiness. Their process has driven them through preliminaries and disclosures, setting them up for the last showdown with the powers that look to disturb the domain's sensitive equilibrium.

Directed by the insight acquired from the core of obscurity and the Tricky Prophet's inestimable experiences, they end up at the nexus of malignance — the focal point from which the shadowy powers radiate. Here, the cloak between the secret world and the malicious domain is at its most slender, and the powers of obscurity assemble strength.

As they advance toward the nexus, the malignant energies pounce upon them with deceptions and dull phantoms, endeavoring to discourage them from their motivation. The perniciousness tries to go after their feelings of trepidation and shortcomings, realizing that any break in their solidarity could mean disaster for the secret world.

Amelia and her colleagues draw upon their recently discovered insight and solidarity, standing up against the perniciousness surge. Every individual from the gathering faces their evil spirits, defying the shadows that have tormented them all through their excursion.

The agonizing magician releases the full degree of his shadowy powers, merging murkiness with light to make a hindrance against the malice. He channels the illustrations of the Dance of Shadows, understanding that dimness can be a wellspring of solidarity when offset with light.

The peculiar designer sends his brilliant manifestations, winding around an embroidery of deceptions to counter the vindictiveness stunts. His creativity turns into an encouraging sign in the murkiness, reminding his mates that resourcefulness and assurance can conquer any test.

The savvy soothsayer calls upon grandiose foreknowledge, unraveling the noxiousness' arrangements and shortcomings. He gives his bits of knowledge to his sidekicks, directing them through the deceptive labyrinth of shadows and deceptions.

Amelia, as the prediction's gatekeeper, bears the heaviness of her obligations. She faces a definitive trial of confidence and mental fortitude, realizing that the shroud should be broken to satisfy the prescience and safeguard the domain's equilibrium.

In a heart-halting second, they face the Shadow Messenger — the noxiousness' encapsulation. The fight that follows is an orchestra of light and shadow, a dance of vast powers that will decide the destiny of the secret world.

As the fight seethes on, they stretch themselves to the edges, their solidarity and assurance powering everything they might do. They understand that they are satisfying the prediction as well as breaking the shroud that isolates the concealed world from dimness itself.

In a strong flood of grandiose energy, Amelia conveys the last blow, breaking the shroud and breaking the malignance's hang on the secret world. Light floods in, dissipating the obscurity that had taken steps to consume everything.

With the cover broken, the secret world is not generally shackled by shadows and malignancy. The Dance of Shadows is reestablished to its actual substance — a sensitive harmony between light and murkiness, creation, and recharging.

Part 23 leaves them with a feeling of win and help, realizing that their penances and solidarity have driven them to this vital second. They comprehend that their excursion to satisfy "The Failed to Remember Prescience" was a mission as well as a grandiose dance of presence — a dance that they are currently sharing with Safeguard.

With the cloak broken and the powers of dimness ousted, they push forward, realizing that their process is not even close to finished. The secret world's equilibrium should be defended interminably, and their obligation to this hallowed obligation turns into their definitive reason.

The breaking of the cloak turns into a pivotal occasion in their excursion — a second that makes way for the prediction's last disclosure. Their journey has carried them to the cliff of predetermination, and they realize that they are the watchmen of the secret world's timeless dance of light and shadow.

Chapter 24: The Light's Triumph

In this stunning section of "The Failed to Remember Prescience," Amelia and her partners stand at the limit of the prediction's victorious satisfaction — the second when the secret world's sensitive dance of light and shadow tracks down its definitive amicability.

Having broken the cloak and ousted the malice that undermined the domain, they presently lounge in the radiance of triumph. The secret world's pith resounds with a newly discovered feeling of harmony and balance, and the reverberations of their process resonate through the enormous embroidery.

As they adventure forward, directed by the insight they have procured, they experience a domain implanted with radiant excellence — a sign of the dance of light and shadow filling together beautifully. The excellence of the secret world's equilibrium leaves them in wonder, and they grasp the holiness of their job as its gatekeepers.

However, amid the victory, they know that the prescience's satisfaction isn't without its last difficulties. The malicious powers might have been expelled, however, there are as yet waiting for leftovers trying to upset the domain's concordance.

Amelia and her buddies realize that their process is incomplete until the prescience is completely understood — the vast disclosure that will reestablish the secret world to its actual embodiment.

As they venture through the brilliant domain, they experience trials of virtue and benevolence — preliminaries that reflect the secret world's dance of light and shadow. The agonizing magician should exhibit how he might interpret the sensitive harmony between his shadowy powers and the light inside him.

The eccentric innovator is tested to relinquish his connection to his developments and embrace the pith of the secret world's creation. He understands that his creations are devices as well as an impression of the domain's inventiveness and interconnectedness.

The savvy diviner faces a preliminary of infinite knowledge, digging into the secret world's past, present, and future — the strings of presence joined with the dance of light and shadow. He appreciates that the prediction's satisfaction requires premonition as well as lowliness despite enormous insights.

Amelia, as well, faces her last preliminary — a trial of immovable responsibility and commitment to the secret world's equilibrium. She should draw upon the strength of her solidarity with her associates, knowing that together, they epitomize the actual pith of the domain's dance of presence.

In the core of the brilliant domain, they experience enormous disclosure — a snapshot of significant knowledge and lucidity. The secret world's mysteries and predictions uncover themselves, winding around an embroidery of vast insight that rises above human cognizance.

In a snapshot of revelation, they grasp the prescience's actual message — the prediction isn't simply an expectation but a core value for protecting the secret world's fragile equilibrium. The prescience's satisfaction lies not in a solitary second but rather in a timeless dance — a dance that requires everlasting carefulness and solidarity.

With the grandiose disclosure engraved on their souls, they realize that they are always bound to the secret world's predetermination. They acknowledge the obligation with lowliness and assurance, realizing that they are the watchmen of the domain's timeless dance of light and shadow.

Section 24 leaves them with a feeling of wonderment and reason — a significant comprehension that they are important for something a lot more significant than themselves. They have turned into the exemplification of the secret world's quintessence — the solidarity of light and shadow, creation, and recharging.

With the prescience's message embraced inside their souls, they press forward, it is everlasting to know that their excursion. The secret world's light and shadow will be in for the rest of the time in motion, and their obligation to its equilibrium turns into their never-ending reason.

The Light's Victory turns into a pivotal occasion in their excursion —
a second that denotes the start of their everlasting hit on the dance
floor with the secret world's pith. They walk connected at the hip
with the dance of light and shadow, realizing that their solidarity
will always defend the domain's fragile harmony.

Chapter 25: The Guardian's Test

In this impactful section of "The Failed to Remember Prescience," Amelia faces an individual preliminary that will decide her value as the genuine gatekeeper of the secret world. As the prediction supports, she comprehends that her responsibility and solidarity with her mates are urgent in protecting the domain's fragile equilibrium.

Directed by the grandiose disclosure and the brilliant domain's insight, Amelia should go through the Gatekeeper's Test — a transitional experience that will stretch her to the edges of her fortitude, shrewdness, and commitment.

The Gatekeeper's Test happens in a consecrated chamber — the core of the radiant domain — where the reverberations of the secret world's presence merge. The chamber is an indication of the domain's pith, permeated with old grandiose energies.

In the chamber, Amelia experiences a progression of preliminaries that address the secret world's dance of light and shadow. Every preliminary mirrors her excursion, the examples she has learned, and the bond she imparts to her mates.

The primary preliminary moves her to go up against her past — the shadows that have tormented her all through her life. Amelia should confront her most profound feelings of trepidation, laments, and questions, embracing her weaknesses with faithful acknowledgment.

The subsequent preliminary tests her determination — the strength of her solidarity with her friends and the domain's inestimable powers. In a significant second, she understands that her process has never been single, and the secret world's dance of presence flourishes with the interconnectedness of every living thing.

The third preliminary is a trial of magnanimity — Amelia should exhibit her obligation to the domain's congruity over her cravings. Her job as the gatekeeper rises above individual desires, and she comprehends that the dance of light and shadow requires penance.

As Amelia persists through every preliminary, she acquires a more profound comprehension of her motivation as the prediction's watchman. She gets a handle on the embodiment of the secret world's equilibrium — the timeless dance that she and her friends should protect.

At the finish of the Watchman's Test, Amelia arrives at a snapshot of significant lucidity and acknowledgment. She comprehends that the watchman's obligation isn't simply to shield the domain from outside dangers yet additionally to support its internal light — the flash of creation and recharging inside every single living being.

In a vital second, she faces a last preliminary — the epitome of the secret world's embodiment. The preliminary appears as a brilliant figure — a heavenly being that exudes the domain's dance of light and shadow.

The heavenly being difficulties Amelia with enormous enigmas — questions that rise above humans getting it. Amelia draws upon the insight she has acquired all through her excursion, answering not with sureness but rather with the lowliness of a gatekeeper dependent on an enormous dance.

Amelia's reaction reverberates with the heavenly being, and at that time, she becomes one with the dance of light and shadow. She understands that the prediction's satisfaction isn't an end but a ceaseless stream — an endless excursion of recharging and balance.

In a stunning peak, Amelia is conceded the Watchman's Approval — an imbuement of enormous energy that ties her everlastingly to the secret world's substance. The domain perceives her as the genuine gatekeeper — the one bound to safeguard the domain's dance of presence.

Section 25 leaves Amelia with a feeling of wonder and obligation — realizing that she currently exemplifies the secret world's pith inside her heart. Her solidarity with her partners is rugged, and they walk together as watchmen of the domain's everlasting dance.

With the Gatekeeper's Favoring, Amelia and her mates push forward, realizing that their process isn't simply a satisfaction of the prescience but a dance of presence with the secret world itself. The domain's sensitive equilibrium is always in their grasp, and their responsibility turns into their life's motivation.

The Watchman's Test turns into a pivotal occasion in Amelia's excursion — a second that cements her job as the secret world's actual gatekeeper. She acknowledges the domain's pith as her own, realizing that she and her partners everlastingly will undoubtedly be its inestimable dance — a dance of light and shadow, creation, and recharging.

Chapter 26: Unraveling the Veiled Enigma

In this section of "The Failed to Remember Prediction," Amelia and her buddies end up drawn further into the core of the secret as they set out on a mission to disentangle the hidden puzzle that covers the secret world. Directed by the Gatekeeper's Favoring and their unfaltering solidarity, they set off on a mission to find the reality behind the grandiose dance of light and shadow.

Their process takes them to old vestiges — remainders of a failed-to-remember development that once held significant information on the secret world's equilibrium. Inside the remains, they experience obscure images and engravings, carved into the stones by a tragically missing hand.

As they translate the puzzling pieces of information, they reveal a progression of tests — preliminaries of intelligence and enormous knowledge that challenge how they might interpret the secret world's pith. The eccentric creator applies his creativity, seeing examples and associations that others miss, while the shrewd diviner digs into the domain's grandiose records to look for antiquated predictions.

Amelia's job as the prediction's gatekeeper turns out to be always critical as she detects that the hidden conundrum holds the way to saving the domain's fragile dance. Her instinct aids her through the tests, drawing upon her solidarity with her partners and the secret world's embodiment.

As they progress through the antiquated vestiges, they experience reverberations of the past — dreams of the human advancement that once flourished together as one with the domain's equilibrium. The dreams uncover the results of disregarding the enormous dance — how irregularity can prompt mayhem and obliteration.

The agonizing magician faces an individual test, considering his previous activities and the shadows that once consumed him. At this time of weakness, his mates' help turns into his anchor, helping him to remember the way he has picked — to safeguard the domain's dance of light and shadow.

The dreams finish in a significant disclosure — a grandiose embroidery that winds around together the secret world's set of experiences and its likely future. They comprehend that the hidden riddle isn't simply a riddle to settle but a portrayal of the secret world's timeless dance — a dance that requires their enduring watchfulness.

With newly discovered astuteness, they rise out of the antiquated remnants, their purpose reinforced and their bond sustained. They realize that the hidden puzzle isn't simply a piece of information to have but an obligation to maintain — an obligation to safeguard the domain's equilibrium and protect its enormous dance.

As they push forward, they experience the leftovers of a malignant faction — a gathering that once looked to take advantage of the secret world's equilibrium for their dull purposes. The religion's presence highlights the significance of their main goal — to guard the domain's quintessence against the individuals who might look to disturb the dance of presence.

85

Amelia and her colleagues face a last conflict with the clique, drawing upon the insight they have acquired and the Gatekeeper's Approval that engages them. In a clash of grandiose powers, they stand joined against, not entirely set in stone to shield the stowed-away world's embodiment from falling into some unacceptable hands.

Part 26 leaves them on the cusp of the hidden conundrum's goal — a disclosure that will shape how they might interpret the secret world's dance of light and shadow. Their solidarity and assurance become their most noteworthy assets as they embrace their job as gatekeepers of the vast dance, depending on the hidden conundrum's insider facts. Reality they look for lies just into the great beyond, and their excursion to safeguard the secret world's offset keeps on unfurling with each step they take.

Chapter 27: The Trials of Illumination

In this charming part of "The Failed to Remember Prescience," Amelia and her buddies end up setting out on a progression of preliminaries that lead them toward a more profound comprehension of the secret world's enlightened dance. Directed by the hidden riddle's disclosures, they set off to go through the Preliminaries of Brightening — a grouping of difficulties that will test their profound experiences and the virtue of their expectations.

The Preliminaries of Light happen in a consecrated haven — a position of ethereal brilliance that radiates the quintessence of the secret world's grandiose dance. As they enter the haven, they feel a significant association with the domain's iridescent energy, and a feeling of stunningness wraps around them.

The primary preliminary, the Preliminary of Lucidity, moves them to face their internal questions and fears. Each sidekick should confront a mirror that mirrors their actual selves — an impression of their past activities and the shadows that once tormented them. Amelia's mates find strength in her steadfast faith in them, supporting each other in tolerating and rising above their difficulties.

The subsequent preliminary, the Preliminary of Solidarity, tests their bond collectively. They should explore through a maze of mirrors that contort reality and make deceptions of division. The genuine test lies in their capacity to trust each other and stay joined despite duplicity.

As they progress through the preliminaries, they experience deceptions of the malicious powers they have looked at previously — the leftovers of the shadow faction and the vindictiveness that once compromised the domain. At these times, they understand that the Preliminaries of Enlightenment are individual tests as well as a portrayal of the secret world's everlasting battle to keep up with its enlightened dance.

The third preliminary, the Preliminary of Enormous Experiences, gives them an inestimable riddle — an embroidery of images that typify the domain's pith. Drawing upon the insight acquired from their excursion, they translate the riddle together, perceiving the interconnectedness of everything in the astronomical dance.

Amidst the preliminaries, Amelia faces her test — a snapshot of uncertainty about her job as the prediction's watchman. At this time of weakness, her partners become her mainstays of solidarity, reaffirming her place as the genuine watchman of the secret world's enlightened dance.

As they close to the finish of the Preliminaries of Enlightenment, they have conceded a dream — a brief look at the secret world's actual potential. They witness an agreeable dance of light and shadow, where each being, each animal, and each part of presence is in wonderful equilibrium.

In this vision, they comprehend that the enlightened dance isn't simply an enormous display but a core value for all life. They understand that the secret world's equilibrium is unpredictably woven into each living soul, and their job as gatekeepers is to secure and sustain this substance.

With the Preliminaries of Light finished, Amelia and her partners rise out of the haven with a restored feeling of direction and solidarity. They realize that the enlightened dance isn't simply a far-off ideal but an unmistakable reality that they should save and maintain.

Section 27 leaves them on the slope of another part of their excursion. The Preliminaries of Enlightenment have gifted them with otherworldly experiences and significant comprehension of the secret world's quintessence. With the hidden mystery's disclosures and the Preliminaries of Enlightenment directing their way, they are prepared to confront the difficulties ahead — to defy the shadows that compromise the domain's sensitive equilibrium and to embrace the secret world's enlightened hit the dance floor with each step they take.

Chapter 28: A New Dawn

In this pivotal section of "The Failed to Remember Prescience," Amelia and her friends stand on the edge of a fresh start —the first light of trust and change. Directed by the insight acquired from the Preliminaries of Enlightenment and the hidden puzzler's disclosures, they get ready to defy the last difficulties that will shape the secret world's predetermination.

As they venture towards the core of the secret world, they witness the principal beams of first light getting through the skyline — an image of the new time that looks for them. The secret world's substance resounds with this inestimable shift, and they feel the domain's energy flooding inside them, engaging all their means.

The excursion drives them to the old Sanctuary of Light — a position of heavenly brilliance where the infinite powers meet. The sanctuary is the epitome of the secret world's enlightened dance, and inside its sacrosanct chambers, they experience the last remainders of the noxious powers that once undermined the domain.

Yet again in a climactic fight, they face the shadows of the past — the malice that tries to disturb the domain's sensitive equilibrium. With the Preliminaries of Enlightenment's experiences and their solidarity as their most noteworthy weapons, they stand resolute notwithstanding obscurity.

Amelia, presently completely receptive to her job as the prescience's watchman, starts to lead the pack in the fight. With each move, she typifies the secret world's substance — the dance of light and shadow, creation, and restoration. Her colleagues lift her, each contributing their novel assets to the battle.

In a snapshot of solidarity, they call the secret world's enormous energies, making a brilliant safeguard that repulses the malice. Their solidarity and enduring dedication to the domain's enlightened dance become a power that rises above individual power.

As the noxiousness withdraws, they arise triumphantly, their bond as colleagues more grounded than at any other time. The fight denotes a defining moment — another sunrise for the secret world, where the enlightened dance will flourish unafraid of malignant interruption.

With the vindictiveness exiled, they face the last phase of their excursion — an inestimable ceremony that will completely stir the secret world's embodiment. Inside the sanctuary's focal chamber, they direct the custom with love and assurance, drawing upon the hidden conundrum's disclosures and the insight acquired from the Preliminaries of Brightening.

As they play out the custom, they feel a flood of infinite energy wrapping them, rising above reality. The secret world's substance vibrates with life, as though recognizing their obligation to its safeguarding and congruity.

In a snapshot of significant clearness, they witness the secret world's enlightened dance unfurling before their eyes. They comprehend that the prescience's satisfaction isn't simply a solitary occasion yet a timeless excursion — a ceaseless dance of light and shadow that they will be for all time a piece of.

Section 28 comes full circle it might be said of wonderment and satisfaction. Amelia and her friends rise out of the sanctuary as the genuine gatekeepers of the secret world's enlightened dance. They walk connected at the hip with the domain's embodiment, realizing that their process isn't simply a satisfaction of the prediction but an everlasting dance of presence.

With the malice ousted and the secret world's embodiment completely stirred, they are presently endowed with the obligation of defending the enlightened dance for a long time into the future. The new day break denotes the start of another period — a future loaded up with vast conceivable outcomes and the timeless concordance of the secret world's embodiment.

Chapter 29: Reckoning with Shadows

In this holding section of "The Failed to Remember Prediction," Amelia and her mates face their most imposing test yet — retribution with the shadows that wait in the secret world. Yet again the new day break has brought a feeling of trust and change, yet the malice isn't vanquished, and its leftovers try to disturb the domain's fragile equilibrium.

As they venture through the secret world, they experience pockets of obscurity — waiting for malignant powers that have taken shelter in the domain's secret corners. The shadows of the past, however, debilitated, still cast an approaching presence, testing their determination and solidarity.

Amelia, as the prescience's gatekeeper, starts to lead the pack in facing the shadows. She comprehends that the enlightened dance requires steady watchfulness and that the malice should be completely uncovered to protect the domain's amicability.

Each sidekick faces their retribution with the shadows, defying their most profound feelings of trepidation and instabilities. The agonizing magician stands up to the obscurity inside himself — an impression of his past battles with his powers and the potential for dimness that exists in him.

The particular designer wrestles with the shadows of uncertainty, scrutinizing his spot in the excursion and his commitment to the domain's equilibrium. With the backing of his sidekicks, he tracks down the solidarity to embrace his part in the vast dance.

The insightful diviner faces a significant issue, battling with the shadows representing things to come — the vulnerability of what lies ahead and the heaviness of infinite information that troubles him. In a snapshot of reflection, he figures out how to find comfort in the present, realizing that the dance of light and shadow requires living at the time.

As they go up against the shadows, they find that the perniciousness draws its solidarity from their questions and fears. They understand that the genuine force of the secret world's quintessence lies in their enduring confidence in the enlightened dance — their obligation to safeguard the domain's sensitive equilibrium.

Amella and her friends should likewise deal with the remainders of the shadow clique — a gathering that once looked to take advantage of the secret world's equilibrium for their dull purposes. In a progression of extraordinary showdowns, they destroy the clique's excess impact, removing the perniciousness at its source.

With the noxiousness completely dealt with, they arise triumphant, realizing that their process isn't just about overcoming obscurity but embracing the dance of light and shadow — the timeless equilibrium that shapes the secret world's pith.

Part 29 leaves them with a recharged feeling of direction and solidarity. They comprehend that the retribution with shadows is not a one-time occasion yet a continuous interaction — an everlasting dance among light and haziness, creation, and recharging.

As they proceed with their excursion, they realize that the secret world's enlightened dance isn't simply a far-off ideal yet an unmistakable reality that they should secure and sustain with each step they take. With the malignance exiled and the shadows gone up against, they walk inseparably with the domain's pith, perpetually dependent on the infinite obligation of protecting its fragile equilibrium.

The retribution with shadows turns into a pivotal occasion in their excursion — a second that sets their obligation to the secret world's enlightened dance. With the hidden puzzler's disclosures and the Preliminaries of Enlightenment directing their way, they are prepared to confront anything challenges that lie ahead, realizing that their solidarity and immovable commitment to the domain's substance will direct them in the everlasting dance of presence.

Chapter 30: The Forgotten Prophecy Fulfilled

In this groundbreaking and climactic part of "The Failed to Remember Prediction," Amelia and her buddies stand at the zenith of their excursion — a finish of preliminaries, disclosures, and development that has driven them to the satisfaction of the old prescience that has directed their way.

As they approach the core of the secret world, they sense a discernible energy — an emanation of inestimable importance that encompasses them. The hidden puzzler's disclosures and the insight acquired from the Preliminaries of Enlightenment have set them up for this last stage — a phase that will decide the fate of the domain's sensitive dance.

Inside the core of the secret world lies the Heavenly Nexus — a hallowed domain where the enormous powers of light and shadow meet. It is here that the prediction's definitive truth will be revealed, and the secret world's pith will track down its last articulation.

Amelia and her friends enter the Divine Nexus with a combination of fear and resolve. The perplexing excursion they have attempted has changed them into genuine watchmen of the secret world's enlightened dance. They stand joined together, realizing that their bond and commitment to the domain's substance are their most noteworthy assets.

In the core of the Divine Nexus, they experience an ethereal presence — an old enormous being that encapsulates the embodiment of the secret world's enlightened dance. The being, with a voice that reverberates with the reverberations of forever, uncovers the prediction's actual reason.

The prediction was not simply a predicting of occasions but rather a vast source of inspiration — a call for Amelia and her allies to embrace their jobs as gatekeepers of the secret world's quintessence. Their process has been an everlasting dance of light and shadow — a dance that rises above reality, forming the actual texture of presence.

As the enormous being gives the prediction's embodiment, they comprehend that their solidarity and dedication to the domain's enlightened dance have been the main thrust behind their excursion. The malice they confronted, the shadows they dealt with, and the preliminaries they went through — all were vital pieces of the dance that has driven them to this second.

With a significant feeling of clearness, Amelia and her buddies understand that the prescience's satisfaction isn't an end yet a fresh start — a timeless pattern of recharging and balance. The secret world's quintessence, as exemplified in the enlightened dance, requires never-ending guardianship — a dance that will go on through the ages.

In an otherworldly second, Amelia and her mates acknowledge their fate as everlasting gatekeepers of the secret world's quintessence. They promise their relentless obligation to the grandiose dance, realizing that their process has become one with the domain's substance.

With the prediction satisfied, they rise out of the Heavenly Nexus, washed in the iridescent brilliance of the secret world's pith. They walk inseparably, not as people, but rather as an enormous power — the encapsulation of the enlightened dance itself.

The secret world's enlightened dance turns into their inheritance — an everlasting demonstration of their commitment, solidarity, and fortitude. As they step into the obscure future, they realize that the dance of light and shadow will keep on directing their way — a dance that will everlastingly shape the predetermination of the secret world and its substance.

In the last section of "The Failed to Remember Prediction," Amelia and her mates track down comfort in their motivation as gatekeepers. Their process has turned into an immortal story — a murmur in the grandiose breeze, perpetually carved in the texture of the secret world's enlightened dance. As they proceed to safeguard and sustain the domain's sensitive equilibrium, they realize that the prescience isn't simply a far-off story of old legend but a living truth — an everlasting dance that will resonate all through the universe forever.

9 798852 479938